A Child's Book of SAINTS

CHRISTOPHER DOYLE

ILLUSTRATED BY MARIA CRISTINA LO CASCIO

Contents

The Saints

From the time of the first followers of Jesus, saints have been those who were considered holy or different—people who wanted to live godly lives. Over time this came to include martyrs (people who had died rather than deny their faith) and anyone whose life was considered outstanding, an inspiration that others might follow.

Although different traditions recognize different individuals as saints, and some traditions count all believers as saints, this collection includes men and women from different times and places who have shared one common goal: to live for God as far as they were able and to put God and other people before themselves.

This small collection of saints illustrates the lives of some special people who have loved and served God. They are included here to inspire us to do the same, in whatever way God calls us.

The Virgin Mary

BORN: UNKNOWN DATE BC, GALILEE
FEAST DAYS: BIRTH ON 8 SEPTEMBER, ANNUNCIATION ON 25 MARCH,
ASSUMPTION ON 15 AUGUST

Mary was obedient to God's call when he chose her to be the mother of the Lord Jesus. She is singled out among all saints as being full of grace.

'I am the Lord's servant!' she said. 'Let it happen as you have said.'

Mary was young and unmarried and risked being made an outcast from her village for being an unmarried mother. But with her fiancé's kindness and with her firm belief that this was God's will, she became the mother of God's Son, Jesus. When the shepherds and wise men from the east visited the new family, Mary thought about all that had happened and about the gifts her new son had received. Years later she was perhaps the first to realize what Jesus' work was all about.

She was a caring parent, supportive of her son as he grew up, and desperately upset as she watched him suffer and die.

Mary is an example of inner strength and humble obedience. She is revered all over the world for being the mother of the Saviour of the world.

Joseph

BORN: UNKNOWN DATE BC, GALILEE

FEAST DAYS: 19 MARCH, 1 MAY

PATRON: THE UNIVERSAL CHURCH, FATHERS, CARPENTERS,
THE DYING AND SOCIAL INJUSTICE

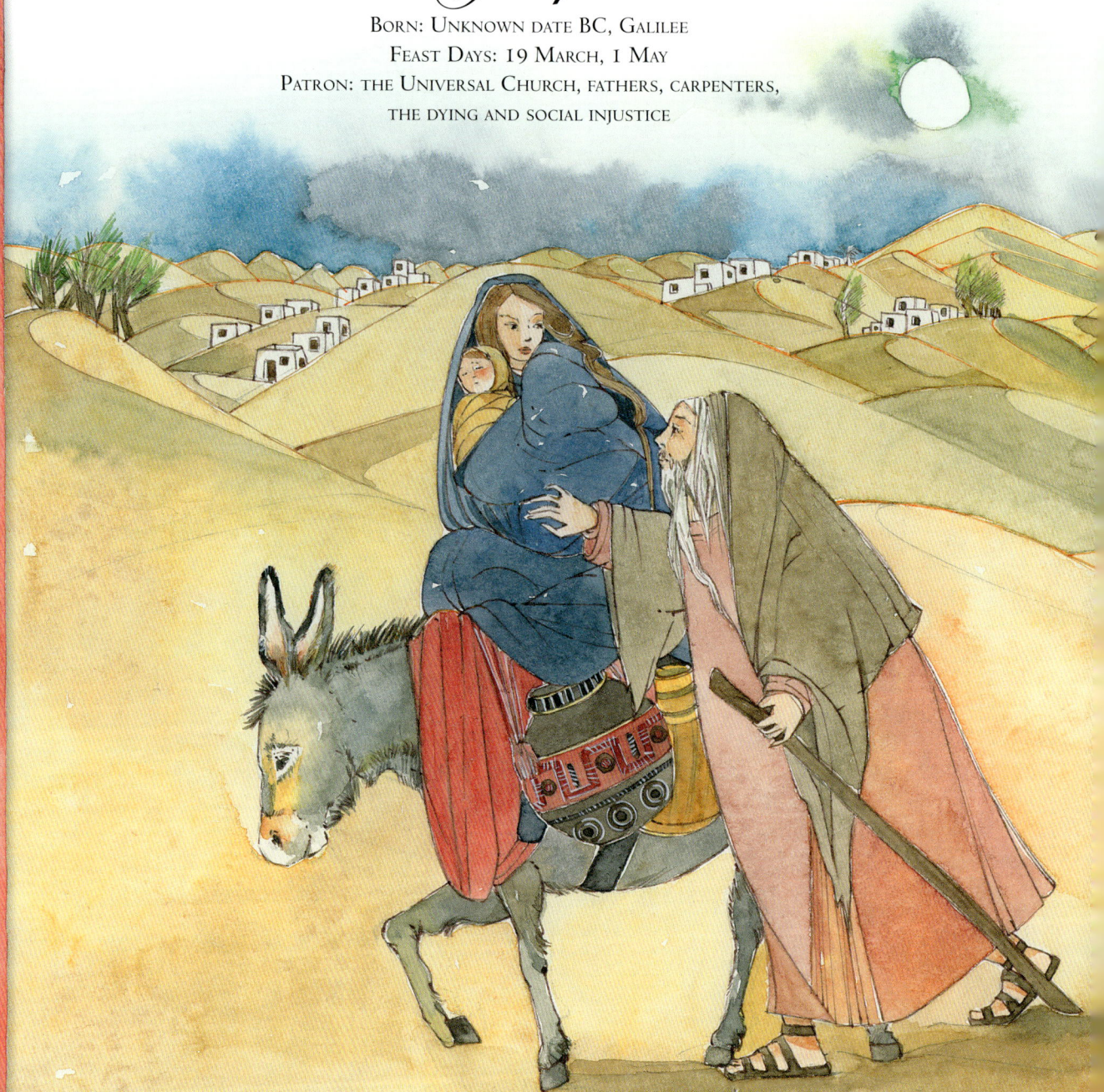

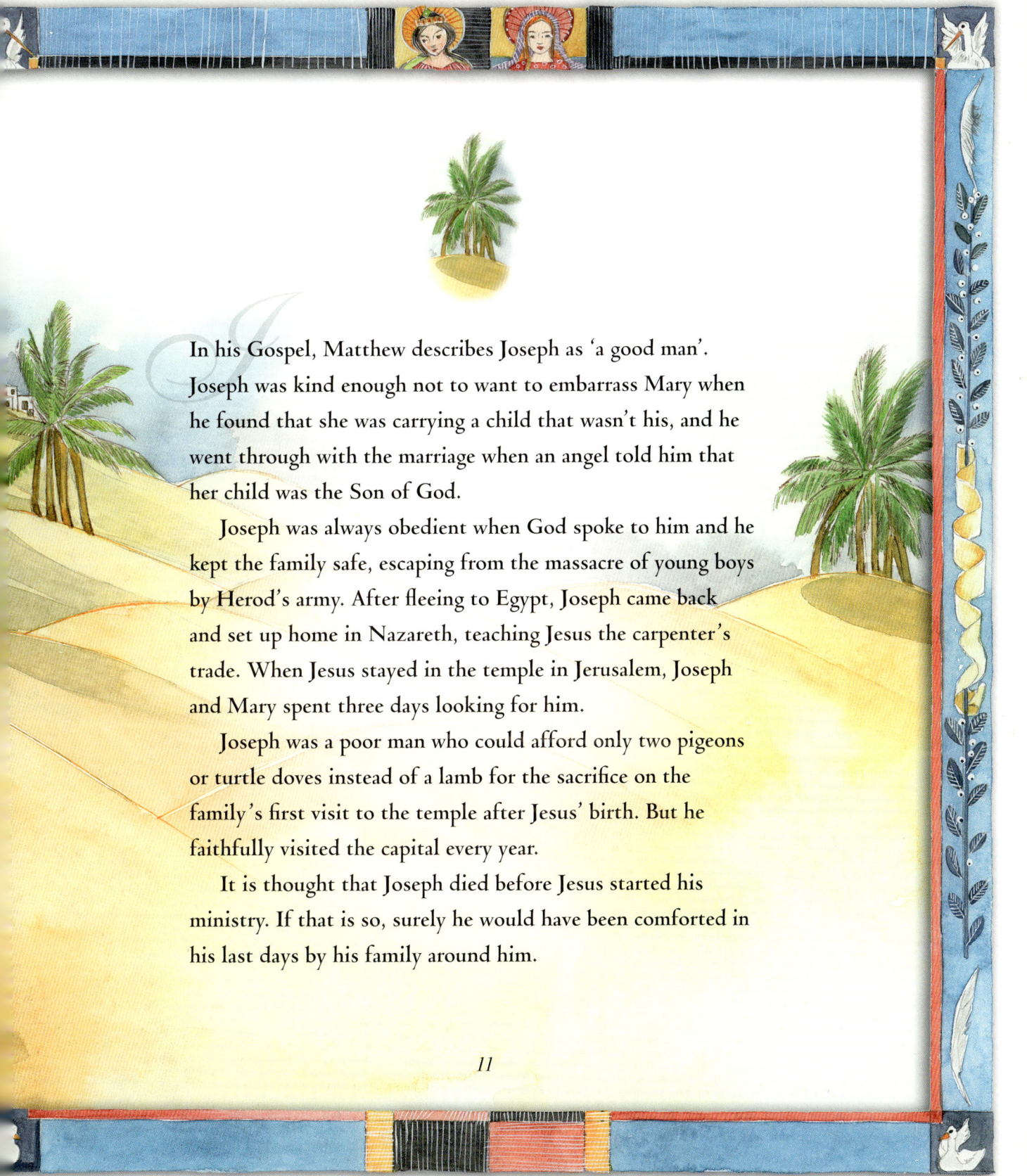

In his Gospel, Matthew describes Joseph as 'a good man'.
Joseph was kind enough not to want to embarrass Mary when
he found that she was carrying a child that wasn't his, and he
went through with the marriage when an angel told him that
her child was the Son of God.

Joseph was always obedient when God spoke to him and he
kept the family safe, escaping from the massacre of young boys
by Herod's army. After fleeing to Egypt, Joseph came back
and set up home in Nazareth, teaching Jesus the carpenter's
trade. When Jesus stayed in the temple in Jerusalem, Joseph
and Mary spent three days looking for him.

Joseph was a poor man who could afford only two pigeons
or turtle doves instead of a lamb for the sacrifice on the
family's first visit to the temple after Jesus' birth. But he
faithfully visited the capital every year.

It is thought that Joseph died before Jesus started his
ministry. If that is so, surely he would have been comforted in
his last days by his family around him.

John the Baptist

BORN: 1ST CENTURY AD, GALILEE
FEAST DAY: 24 JUNE

When people came out into the wilderness to see John, dirty and wild-looking, dressed in animal skins, he didn't know that his work was nearly over.

'Turn back to God and be baptized! Then your sins will be forgiven,' he declared.

John told everyone who would listen that Jesus was coming, a man much greater than he, and that they should take notice of all he said.

John's birth had been miraculous. His mother had been far too old to have a baby. His father, Zechariah, served in the temple. He was given special instructions from an angel that visited him there. When the child was born, Zechariah was insistent that they call him John. The old couple didn't realize then that their son was to become the prophet who would prepare the way for the start of Jesus' ministry.

Only when Jesus waded into the River Jordan did John realize the importance of the event and baptize him as instructed.

John died at the request of King Herod's stepdaughter who asked for his head on a plate as a present. John's work was over, but the symbolic washing of people still goes on today in the ceremony of baptism.

Matthew

BORN: 1ST CENTURY AD, PALESTINE
FEAST DAY: 21 September
PATRON: BANKERS

Matthew, the son of Alpheus, wrote the Gospel that bears his name. It is the 'doorway' into the New Testament. It links what the prophets foretold about Jesus in the Old Testament to the life of Jesus at the start of the New Testament. Matthew often explains some of the events in Jesus' life as fulfilling those prophesies.

Jesus called Matthew to be a disciple while he was about his work as a tax collector in Capernaum. He was one of the twelve men who lived and worked with Jesus for the three years of his ministry. Matthew saw blind people given their sight, ate bread and fish with the crowd of 5000, experienced the calming of the storm on the lake, heard Jesus' parables firsthand and saw Jesus after the resurrection.

When Herod Agrippa persecuted the early Christians, Matthew left Israel. He may have gone to Ethiopia or Parthia or Persia. But one thing is sure: he knew for himself, and left us a true message, that Jesus was the Son of God.

Luke

BORN: 1ST CENTURY AD, ANTIOCH, TURKEY
FEAST DAY: 18 OCTOBER
PATRON: PHYSICIANS AND SURGEONS

Luke, one of Paul's travelling companions from his second missionary journey, is described as 'our dear doctor'. It is thought that he was a slave who was educated so that he could minister to the family he served. He was not an eyewitness to Jesus' ministry but he wrote a Gospel based on the accounts of other eyewitnesses and he also wrote the Acts of the Apostles.

The Gospel Luke wrote often mentions poor people and those who need forgiveness, as well as containing more of the healing miracles than the Gospels of Matthew, Mark or John.

Luke's is the only Gospel that gives a full account of Jesus' birth. He tells how Jesus was born into an ordinary family and how his birth took place in a stable because there was no room in the inn. Luke is also the only Gospel writer who mentions the man with leprosy who said thank you, and the parables of the good Samaritan and the prodigal son.

Luke showed his love for poor people and his respect for women and had no doubt that Jesus came to offer his love and mercy to everyone, whoever they were and whatever their background.

Peter

BORN: 1ST CENTURY AD, PALESTINE
FEAST DAY: 29 JUNE

Peter was described by Jesus as the rock upon which Jesus would build the church; the man who would inspire others to follow Jesus and join together to follow Jesus' teachings. But when Jesus was on trial, Peter showed his weaker, human side and denied that he even knew his master. Peter often spoke or acted first and thought about it afterwards, once even prompting Jesus to say, 'Satan, get away from me!'

Peter was a solid, no-nonsense man. Originally called Simon, he left the family fishing business along with his brother Andrew and followed Jesus faithfully for three years. In spite of his faults, Peter's simple and straightforward approach made him the ideal person to lead the church in its early years. It was Peter who, with the power of the Holy Spirit, was the first to address the crowd at Pentecost.

Peter died in Rome, condemned by the Emperor Nero to be crucified.

'Please,' he asked, 'if I am to be crucified, let it be upside down. I am unworthy to suffer in the same way Jesus did.'

Paul

BORN: 1ST CENTURY AD, TARSUS, TURKEY
FEAST DAY: 25 JANUARY

It would be difficult to find a man more wholehearted in what he believed in than Paul.

Before he met Jesus, Paul was violently opposed to everything the new 'Christians' believed. He stood by and watched as Stephen was stoned to death. He set out on a journey to round up and kill more of the early Christians. But Paul was changed by his meeting with Jesus on the road to Damascus.

'Saul,' (for that was his name in those days) 'why are you so cruel to me?'

No one could see where the voice came from and Paul himself was blinded by a flash of lightning. In that moment he understood that Jesus was speaking to him.

Paul knew that this life-changing event meant great news, not only for himself and the Jewish people, but also for all those outside the Jewish faith. Spreading the message that Jesus forgives us for the wrong we do was now Paul's life's work. He set off on many journeys to the countries around the eastern Mediterranean. When he was taken to Rome as a prisoner, he wrote to his old friends, instructing them in the way they should live their lives for Jesus. Paul's many teachings form the basis of what the church still instructs today.

From tentmaker to travelling teacher, persecutor to preacher, God used the enthusiastic and controversial Paul for good in the Christian church.

Stephen

BORN: 1ST CENTURY AD, PALESTINE
FEAST DAY: 26 DECEMBER
PATRON: DEACONS, HEADACHES, HORSES, COFFIN MAKERS AND MASONS

Stephen was the first Christian martyr. He had been chosen as one of the deacons that the disciples had appointed to help them keep account of the possessions they shared. They needed someone trustworthy to organize the gifts to people who were poor and needy—and Stephen was that man.

But Stephen proved also to be a gifted preacher. When he was arrested on false accusations he had to answer to the Jewish court. He used the opportunity to explain how they had murdered Jesus, the person foretold from the time of the prophets, through their unbelief.

The priests were so furious that they dragged Stephen out of the city. His angelic face angered them even more. As the stones rained down on him he looked up to see Jesus and the angels calling him.

Stephen died because he would not give up his belief in Jesus. His dying words echoed those of Jesus from the cross: 'Lord, don't blame them for what they have done.'

Nicholas

BORN: c AD 270, PATARA, LYCIA, TURKEY
FEAST DAY: 6 DECEMBER
PATRON: CHILDREN, PAWNBROKERS, SAILORS,
BAKERS, RUSSIA, GREECE AND SEVERAL SEA PORTS

'What are we to do?' cried the men. Wind and waves lashed their ship, threatening to capsize her.

Legend has it that, from nowhere, St Nicholas appeared. He held out his hand over the sea; the gale died down and all was calm again.

Nicholas came from a wealthy family but his parents taught him to share. When he grew older he heard about a man who had lost all his money just before his three daughters were to be married. The man thought he would have to sell the girls into slavery but, the following morning, a bag of gold lay on the floor—Nicholas had thrown it in through the window during the night. He did the same on the following two nights, saving the family. Pawnbrokers use the sign of three balls, representing the bags of gold, outside their shops.

St Nicholas is the man upon whom Santa Claus is based—the person who makes gifts for children and delivers them at Christmas, around the time when Jesus' birth is celebrated.

Alban

BORN: 3RD CENTURY AD, VERULAMIUM, ENGLAND
FEAST DAY: 22 JUNE

Alban lived in England when it was ruled by the Roman Empire and, like other Roman citizens, he worshipped the Roman gods.

One day Alban took pity on a Christian priest who was on the run from the Roman authorities in the town of Verulamium. Alban hid the priest in his house for a few days. During that time Alban listened to the priest's teaching about Jesus. Alban began to believe in God for himself and became a Christian.

'Give me your clothes,' Alban said to the priest when the soldiers came for him. 'Escape through the back door and I'll pretend to be you.'

When Alban appeared at the front of the house, the plan was discovered and the Roman guards arrested him. He was condemned to death for tricking the governor—and for refusing to worship the Roman gods. His executioner marched Alban across the fields to the top of a nearby hill. But on the way Alban told his guard all about Jesus and the guard also became a Christian. When they reached the place of execution the guard refused to behead Alban. Another executioner had to be found before both Alban and the first guard were beheaded!

George

BORN: 3RD CENTURY AD, NICODEMIA, BITHYNIA

FEAST DAY: 23 APRIL

PATRON: ENGLAND

The soldiers of the crusade who were encamped around Jerusalem looked up in awe. Who was this phantom figure striding ahead of them against the Saracen army? George was the inspiration that led them into battle.

George was a Christian who grew up in Turkey in the third century after Christ's birth. He moved to Israel with his mother and later enlisted in the Roman army. It was when Emperor Diocletian decided to persecute Christians that George stood up to be counted among them. In spite of horrible torture he refused to deny Jesus and worship the Roman gods. For his defiance of the Emperor and for his faith in Jesus, he was beheaded.

Many stories grew up about George, including his slaying of a dragon to rescue a princess. Edward III of England made George patron of the new order of knighthood, the Order of the Garter. In 1940 King George VI instituted the George Cross, a medal for civilians who had shown outstanding bravery. It bears the image of the courageous St George… slaying a dragon.

Martin

BORN: AD 316, HUNGARY
FEAST DAY: 11 NOVEMBER
PATRON: FRANCE AND SOLDIERS

Martin was only ten years old when he went secretly to the church in what is modern-day Hungary. He went to learn more about God, away from the disapproving eyes of his parents. But before Martin could be baptized, he was forced to join the Roman cavalry and moved to France.

One winter's day, as he rode out of the city of Amiens in his armour, he noticed a beggar dressed in rags, his skin blue with the cold. Martin stopped his horse and took off his cloak. With one stroke of his sword, Martin split the cloak in two.

'Here you are, old man,' said Martin, handing the beggar half his cloak, 'warm yourself with this.'

That night, Martin dreamed that it was Jesus who was wearing half his cloak. In the morning the cavalryman asked a priest to baptize him. Martin then left the cavalry, declaring that he had to fight in God's army.

Martin led a simple life as a hermit, later setting up a monastery. When he died, his body was taken to Tours where pilgrims would visit his tomb.

Jerome

BORN: AD 347, STRIDON, DALMATIA
FEAST DAY: 30 SEPTEMBER
PATRON: TRANSLATORS, LIBRARIANS, ENCYCLOPEDISTS

Jerome grew up in Asia Minor, near Dalmatia. He went to Rome in his early teenage years to study language and grammar.

He suffered several bouts of illness, and during one of these he had a vision that led him to devote himself more to learning about Christianity and to studying Christian writings. He learned the Jewish language and exchanged letters with Jewish Christians in Antioch. In Rome, Jerome was ordained as a priest and soon became an invaluable helper of Pope Damasus I.

Later, back in Antioch, in a monastery set up by some of his friends, Jerome devoted his time to writing. He completed translations of the Bible and several commentaries on different Bible passages. Jerome was responsible for the Vulgate Bible, a Latin Bible translated from the Hebrew writings, which was the main Bible translation for hundreds of years. One of his sayings was that ignorance of the scriptures is ignorance of Christ.

Jerome died near Bethlehem aged over 70. One story tells of the time he pulled a thorn out of a lion's paw, because the creature was in so much pain, and so he is often pictured with a lion.

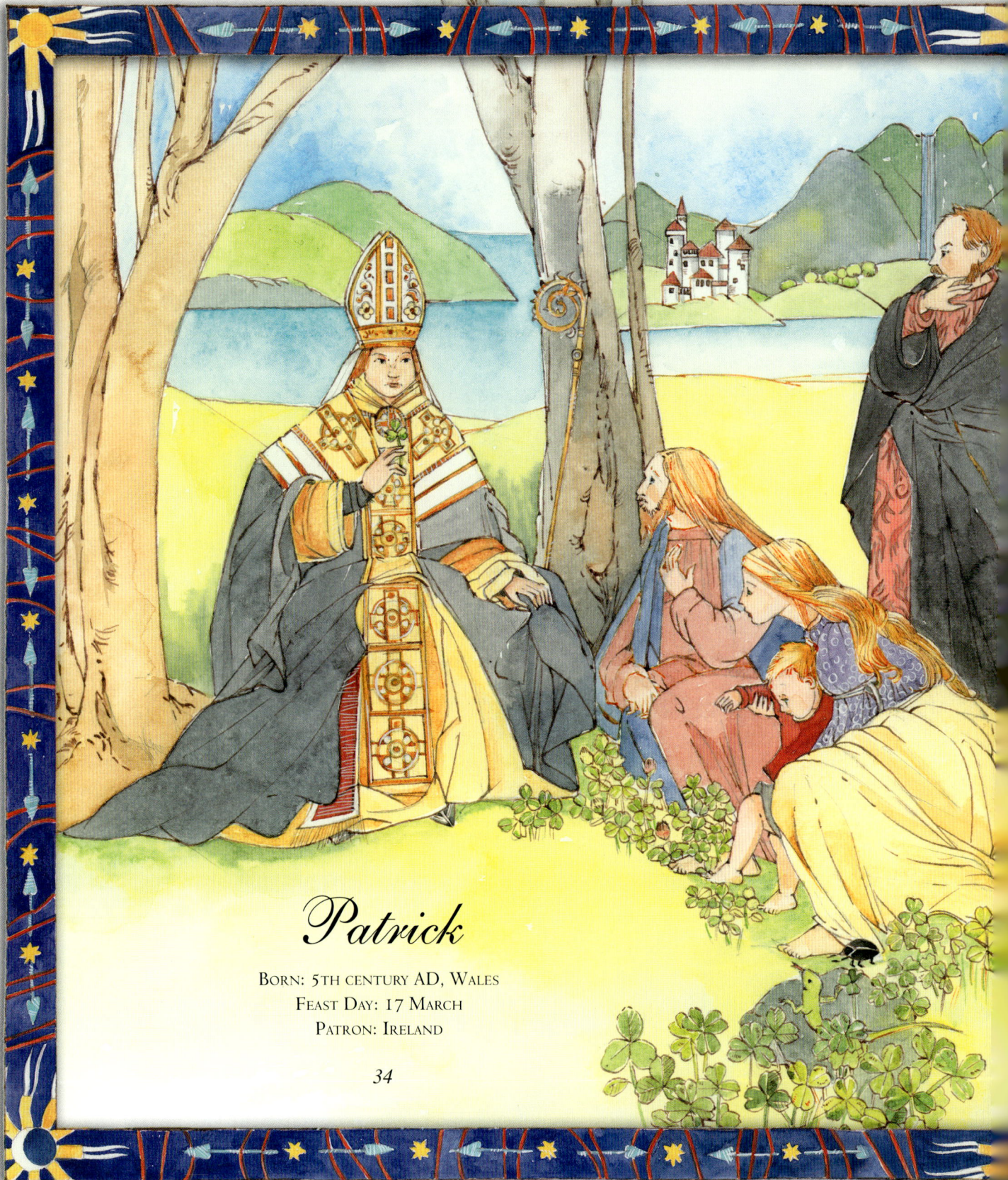

Patrick

BORN: 5TH CENTURY AD, WALES
FEAST DAY: 17 MARCH
PATRON: IRELAND

Although adopted as the patron saint of Ireland, Patrick was born in Wales.

Back in his native country he had not known God at all. He had been captured by pirates as a teenager and forced to work in Ireland. There he came to understand that God was keeping him safe and well until the time when he would return as a missionary, to tell the people about God.

Patrick made his escape by stowing away in a boat, vowing to become a priest if he became a free man. Later, God spoke to him in a dream, calling him back to work in the place where he had been a slave.

'What is the Trinity?' Patrick asked. 'How can God, Jesus and the Holy Spirit be three people but one person? Well, here is the same thing.' Between his fingers Patrick held the delicate stem of a shamrock leaf. It was one leaf but seemed to be made of three leaves. 'You see, three parts but they make up one leaf,' he said.

Boniface

BORN: AD 673, CREDITON, ENGLAND
FEAST DAY: 5 JUNE
PATRON: THE NETHERLANDS, GERMANY, BREWERS,
TAILORS, FILE CUTTERS, WORLD YOUTH DAY

Boniface was called Wynfrith at his birth in the Devonshire town of Crediton, England. After training as a monk and receiving his new name, he was sent by the Pope to Germany.

The people of Germany at this time worshipped the pagan god of thunder and believed that the oak tree was sacred. Boniface swung an axe into a tree trunk until, with a creak and a crash, the mighty oak toppled and fell.

'You said Thor would strike me down if I were to fell the tree…' Boniface said to the watching crowd. But there was no lightning bolt; nothing happened. The tribesmen were so amazed that they listened to the message about Jesus that Boniface had come to preach. In the roots of the oak there grew a small fir tree. Boniface gave the new Christians something to remember about Jesus.

'You use this wood to build your homes; let Christ be at the centre of your households. Its leaves remain green all year; let Christ be your constant light. Its branches reach out to embrace and its top points to heaven; let Christ be both your comfort and your guide.'

Boniface set up many new churches in his adopted country and never returned to his home.

Francis of Assisi

BORN: 26 SEPTEMBER 1181, ASSISI, UMBRIA, ITALY
FEAST DAY: 4 OCTOBER
PATRON: BIRDS AND ANIMALS

Many people all over the world set up a crib scene at Christmas. The tradition started with St Francis, who set up such a scene in Greccio village church with real animals, and villagers playing the parts of Mary and Joseph cradling a baby. Francis wanted people to see how Jesus had come into the world as a poor person, just like themselves.

Francis had not been poor. As the son of a rich merchant, he had received a good education and joined the army, fighting many battles. When he saw that this was not the life God wanted him to lead, he used his money to rebuild the ruined chapel of St Damian in Assisi. Then he gave his clothes to his father, telling him he would be married to 'Lady Poverty'.

Francis loved nature, and legend has it that he befriended birds and animals—even taming a wolf that had been killing goats.

Determined to live life simply, Francis started an order of monks called the Franciscans. Like Francis, each monk vows to give up his possessions and dresses in a simple brown tunic or habit.

Anthony

BORN: 1195, LISBON, PORTUGAL
FEAST DAY: 13 JUNE
PATRON: LOST ITEMS

St Anthony's great gift was to preach, encouraging people to put their trust in Jesus.

Born into a rich family, and given the name Ferdinand, he joined the Augustinian order of monks. He became convinced he should go to North Africa after some Franciscan monks he had met were killed for their faith there.

Ferdinand became a Franciscan and travelled to Morocco under the name Anthony, but became so ill he had to return. On the way back to Portugal his ship ran into a storm and was blown off course. Anthony, now in very poor health, was offered a home in a monastery in Italy, where he worked in the kitchens.

One day some visitors came to be ordained and Anthony was given the task of preaching at the ceremony. His sermon showed everyone that he had found his gift. He travelled all over Italy and into France where people were amazed at his teaching.

There was one famous occasion, however, when he was ridiculed in Padua. Anthony turned to some fish in a river and preached to them instead about the God who had made them and cared for them. To everyone's amazement, the fish lifted their heads above the water as if to listen while he spoke.

Ignatius Loyola

BORN: 24 DECEMBER 1491, LOYOLA, GUIPÚZCOA, SPAIN
FEAST DAY: 31 JULY
PATRON: SPIRITUAL EXERCISES, BASQUE COUNTRY, DIOCESES OF DONOSTIA AND BILBAO, SPAIN, JESUITS, MILITARY ORDINARIATE OF THE PHILIPPINES, SOCIETY OF JESUS, SOLDIERS, BISCAY

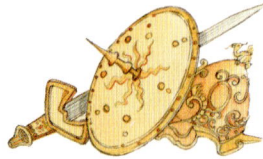

As a young man, Ignatius was a brave soldier. But one day a canon ball injured both his legs. He had to undergo painful operations and in the months of recovery he was given books to read about the life of Jesus and the lives of saints.

Ignatius was inspired by all he read. He gave up his sword and armour and spent three days confessing all his sins to Mary before going to the Holy Land to tell others about Jesus.

When Ignatius returned to study in Spain and France, he crafted his 'Spiritual Exercises', a set of meditations and prayers to help people find their way in the Christian life. Then he went to Rome to see what Pope Paul III wanted him to do next.

It was then that he and some friends founded the Society of Jesus or the 'Jesuits'. They vowed to go wherever they were sent and do whatever the Pope would have them do in the service of others, whether rich or poor. Ignatius was voted to be the first leader, or Superior General, of the Jesuits. The order set up many Jesuit colleges around the world to train men for the priesthood.

Innocent

BORN: 26 AUGUST 1797, IRKUTSK, RUSSIA
FEAST DAYS: 31 MARCH AND 6 OCTOBER

Icy water splashed over the bow of the canoe as Father Ivan battled the waves on the stormy ocean, on yet another trip to islands off the coast of Alaska to visit members of his far-flung diocese.

The Russian Orthodox priest had moved from his home in Irkutsk, in the depths of Siberian Russia, to live in these islands. Life was harsh but with help from local people he was able to build a church. He learnt the local languages and translated portions of the Bible and other church material for the people.

Ivan was on a visit to mainland Russia reporting on his activities when he heard that his wife had died in their home in Sitka. During his stay in Russia he decided to become a monk, taking the name Innocent.

Innocent returned to the islands to become bishop of a huge diocese that spread from mainland Russia to his beloved Aleutian Islands. He continued to translate the Bible into local languages and made many missionary journeys into the remote areas. He was determined that as many as possible of his charges should be able to read for themselves about the Lord they worshipped.

John Bosco

BORN: 16 AUGUST 1815, PIEDMONT, ITALY

FEAST DAY: 31 JANUARY

PATRON: CHRISTIAN APPRENTICES, EDITORS, PUBLISHERS, SCHOOLCHILDREN, YOUNG PEOPLE

Through love, kindness and encouragement, John Bosco cared for and trained many wild young boys from the streets of Italy.

John's father had died when he was only two years old and his family were poor. He had worked hard to be able to study and once, while working as a shepherd boy, he had dreamed that he was surrounded by boys fighting and misbehaving. A man with a kindly face took him to one side and explained that John would have to control them not by beating them but with kindness. Now, in the schools he set up through the Salesian Society, his dream had come true.

He had been moved to help children after visiting prisons and seeing how badly young people were treated there. He started an 'Oratory', a travelling school for street boys, which eventually settled in the Italian city of Turin. John's mother came to help him look after the boys while he supervised their education.

Over the years members of the Salesian Society travelled to other parts of the world using John's teaching methods. For his outstanding work with young people, John Bosco is known in the church as the 'Father and Teacher of Youth'.

Bernadette

BORN: 7 JANUARY 1844, LOURDES, FRANCE
FEAST DAY: 16 APRIL
PATRON: THOSE WHO ARE UNWELL, POVERTY, LOURDES, SHEPHERDS

Bernadette was 14 when she had the first of 18 visions of Mary at Lourdes.

The first happened when she was sent out one day to fetch firewood. As she bent down she heard a rustling noise and looked up to see a small young woman dressed in white with a blue girdle and a golden rose on each foot.

During one of her visions, the young woman told her to drink water from the spring under the rock.

'I can see no spring,' said Bernadette. 'The ground is dry.' But when Bernadette dug into the soil with her hands, water flowed freely.

The visions stopped as suddenly as they had begun. Bernadette disliked the attention she received and she moved to the town of Nevers to join the Sisters of Charity there.

Bernadette was questioned by officials from the church and the French government many times and in great depth about her visions. She was adamant about what she had seen. She asked the priest to build a chapel at the site of the visions and millions of people have visited Lourdes to discover the healing properties of the waters that Bernadette uncovered.

Therese of Lisieux

BORN: 2 JANUARY 1873, ALENÇON, NORMANDY, FRANCE
FEAST DAY: 1 OCTOBER
PATRON: THE MISSIONS

Therese entered a Carmelite order when she was only 15. It was a different life from her childhood where she had been treated like a little princess by her father and sisters. Then, tears and tantrums followed if she didn't have her own way! But one day, as she lay ill in bed, she prayed and was convinced she saw Mary smile at her. This was the beginning of the change that overcame her.

Therese wanted to work for God. But she was not allowed out of the closed community or able to do any 'great' things. Therese realized that God wanted her to accept her position and every trouble that came to her without question and that it was in every small thing we do that we can serve God. She learned humility. She no longer complained; she smiled at people she didn't like, and even took the blame for breaking a vase when it wasn't her fault.

Therese wrote down all that she learned and, although she died of tuberculosis aged only 24, her writings have inspired many to live their lives accepting themselves and being the person God wants them to be.

Frances Xavier Cabrini

BORN: 15 JULY 1850, SANT ANGELO, LOMBARDY, ITALY
FEAST DAY: 22 DECEMBER
PATRON: IMMIGRANTS AND HOSPITAL ADMINISTRATORS

'China: that is where I feel my mission lies,' Maria Francesca Cabrini told the Pope.

It had taken a struggle to reach this far but the frail nun had God-given strength in a body weakened by premature birth and childhood illness.

She had become a teacher in an orphanage in her native Lombardy and, when the orphanage closed, Maria Francesca set up her own community. With the Pope's blessing she had set up two convents in Rome. But instead of sending her to the Far East, the Pope sent Sister Maria Frances to New York—the far west! Also known as Mother Cabrini, the determined nun raised money for a house to use as a convent and orphanage and soon afterwards opened a hospital. She became a naturalized American citizen and, during the next 28 years of her life, opened many more hospitals, convents, orphanages and schools in the name of her order, the Missionary Sisters of the Sacred Heart, throughout the USA, South America and Europe.

Mother Cabrini died in 1917 and in 1946 was the first American citizen to be canonized.

Maximilian Kolbe

BORN: 7 JAN 1894, ZDUNSKA WOLA, POLAND
FEAST DAY: 14 AUGUST
PATRON: THE PRO-LIFE MOVEMENT, DRUG ADDICTS, FAMILIES, AMATEUR RADIO

Baptized Raymond, Maximilian was a difficult child but took up holy orders after seeing a vision of Mary. Although his teachers thought he would become a great scientist, he used his skills to organize the printing of a Catholic newspaper and even published a magazine in Japanese while building a monastery near Nagasaki. But back in Poland in 1941, Maximilian was arrested for hiding people of Jewish faith. He was sent to Auschwitz, the feared concentration camp.

'A prisoner has escaped!' declared the commandant. 'Now ten of you must die as punishment.'

The chosen prisoners were being marched away when one cried out, 'My wife and children—I shall never see them again!'

Maximilian stepped forward. 'Let me take his place,' he said.

Almost three weeks later, Maximilian was the only prisoner left alive in that dank starvation cell. He had encouraged others by singing hymns and saying prayers, but the guards put him to death with an injection of poison.

A priest, newspaper publisher, scientist, radio presenter and a missionary, Maximilian Kolbe aimed in every way to bring people to a belief in Christ. His courage and devotion to Christ were all outstanding.

Pier Giorgio Frassati

BORN: 6 APRIL 1901 TURIN, ITALY
FEAST DAY: 4 JULY

Pier Giorgio, a wonderful skier, athlete and mountain climber, was also a very devout Christian who gave time and money to help poor people.

Pier's father was a wealthy newspaper owner, but any pocket money Pier received he always gave away to help those less fortunate. He often ran home, having given away his train fare. One day a poor mother and child came to the door to beg.

'I see you have no shoes, little one,' noted Pier Giorgio. 'Here, take mine!'

When Pier Giorgio graduated, his father offered him a present of a car or some money. The young man took the money and promptly gave it away. He made sure a poor old woman had a room in which to stay after she was evicted from her flat. He provided a bed for someone who was unwell and he supported three children whose father had died. And almost every day he helped at services of Holy Communion and spent hours in prayer.

Pier Giorgio contracted poliomyelitis when he was 24 and died within a few weeks. At his funeral, thousands lined the streets.

Mother Teresa

BORN: 27 AUGUST 1910, SKOPJE, REPUBLIC OF MACEDONIA
BEATIFIED: 19 OCTOBER 2003
FEAST DAY: 5 SEPTEMBER

Agnes Gonxha Bojaxhiu was fascinated by the lives of the missionaries. She joined the Sisters of Loreto when she was 18 and moved to India in 1929, taking the name Teresa after the saint from Lisieux, the patron of missionaries.

Teresa was sure God was calling her to work among poor people. She wore the simple white chira decorated with a blue border, and moved to the slums of Calcutta. Her Missionaries of Charity cared for 'all those people who feel unwanted, unloved, uncared for throughout society'.

Later in her life Mother Teresa was not afraid to travel to war-torn countries to rescue children and adults caught up in the fighting and she was awarded the Nobel Peace Prize in 1979. Instead of the usual ceremonial banquet, she asked for the money that would have been spent on it to be sent to help poor people in India.

Mother Teresa died in 1997 in Calcutta, the city in which she had spent over 60 years working with those who lived with poverty and disease.

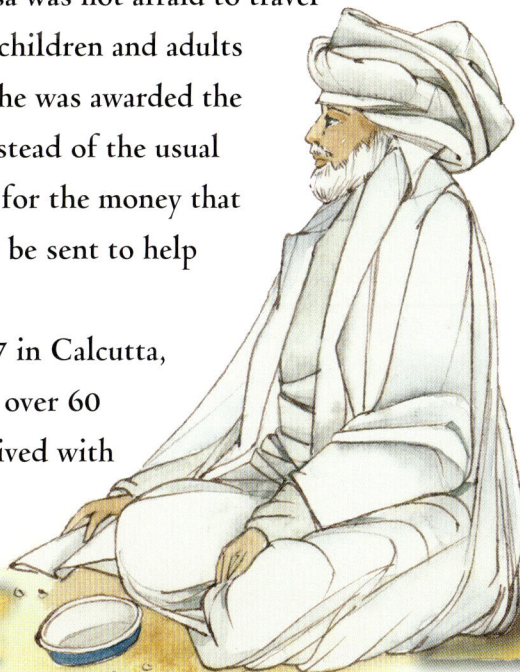

59

Index of Saints

Published by
The Bible Reading Fellowship, 15 The Chambers, Vineyard
Abingdon, OX14 3FE United Kingdom
Tel: +44 (0) 1865 319700
Email: enquiries@brf.org.uk
Website: www.brf.org.uk

ISBN 978 1 84101 682 5
First edition 2009

Copyright © 2009 Anno Domini Publishing Services
Book House, Orchard Mews, 18 High Street, Tring, Herts HP23 5AH United Kingdom

Text copyright © 2009 Christopher Doyle
Illustrations copyright © 2009 Maria Cristina Lo Cascio
Publishing Director Annette Reynolds
Editor Nicola Bull
Art Director Gerald Rogers
Pre-production Krystyna Kowalska Hewitt
Production John Laister

A catalogue record for this book is available from the British Library.

Printed by Oriental Press